Eating

Gwenyth Swain

Carolrhoda Books, Inc./Minneapolis

For Vinnie, who loves to eat!

To find out more about the pictures in this book, turn to page 22.
To find out more about sharing this book with children, turn to page 24.

The photographs in this book are reproduced through the courtesy of: Stephen Graham Photography, front cover; ©Elaine Little/World Photo Images, back cover, pp. 9, 18; IPS, p. 1; ©Gerald Cubitt, pp. 3, 20; Sharon Wilharm, p. 4; ©TRIP/C.C., p. 5; ©TRIP/H. Rogers, p. 6; ©TRIP/M. Peters, p. 7; ELCA photo. Used by permission of Augsburg Fortress, p. 8; David Chittenden, p. 10; George Washington Carver National Monument, National Parks Service, p. 11; SeaQuest Cruises, p. 12; ©TRIP/F. Good, p. 13; F. Botts/FAO, p. 14; Eliot Elisofon, Eliot Elisofon Archives, National Museum of African Art, Smithsonian Institution, p. 15; Jeff Greenberg, p. 16; WPF/FAO photo by F. Mattioli, p. 17; ©Lyn Hancock, p. 19; ©John Elk, p. 21.

This book is available in two editions:
Library binding by Carolrhoda Books, Inc., a division of Lerner Publishing Group
Soft cover by First Avenue Editions, an imprint of Lerner Publishing Group
241 First Avenue North, Minneapolis, MN 55401 U.S.A.

Website address: www.lernerbooks.com

Library of Congress Cataloging-In-Publication Data

Swain, Gwenyth, 1961–
  Eating / by Gwenyth Swain.
    p. cm. — (Small world)
  Includes index.
  Summary: In photographs and rhyming text, describes the foods and eating customs of people around the world.
  ISBN 1-57505-257-1 (lib. bdg. : alk. paper) 1-57505-369-1 (pbk. : alk. paper)
  1. Food—Juvenile literature. 2. Food habits—Juvenile literature. 3. English language—Rhymes—Juvenile literature. [1. Food habits. 2. Food.] I. Title. II. Series: Small world (Minneapolis, Minn.)
TX355.S93 1999
641.3—dc21   98-3253

Manufactured in the United States of America
5 6 7 8 9 10 – JR – 09 08 07 06 05 04

It's time for breakfast.
What will you eat?

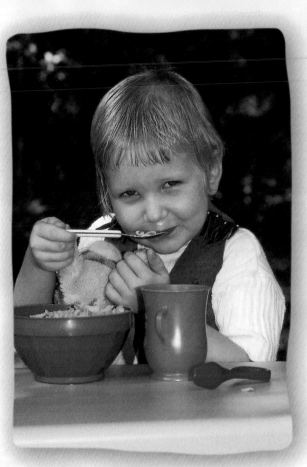

Will you put milk on cornflakes?

Or will you grab something sweet?

Eating can be messy.

It's also fun to do.

Wash your hands. Give thanks.

Then dig into your food!

You can eat at a table,

on the ground,

or on the run.

But before you can eat,
there's a lot to be done.

Buy food or grow it.

Then, pound it or sort it.

Chop it, then stir it.

Grill it on a fire or cook it in a pot.

Food tastes great—sometimes hot,
sometimes not.

When you share a meal,
you share good tastes and good times.

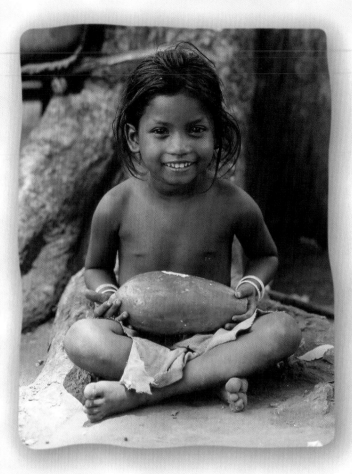

Sit right down. Take a big bite!

Eating will make you feel just right.

More about the Pictures

Front cover: Peanut butter on bread makes for fun but messy eating for this boy in Ann Arbor, Michigan.

Back cover: A girl in the Philippines carries a big bowl full of bananas.

Page 1: Two boys in Guyana, in South America, slurp flavored ice cones.

Page 3: For this toddler in northern India, breakfast starts with a bottle of milk.

Page 4: This young girl in Cantonment, Florida, begins the day with a bowl of cornflakes.

Page 5: At a market in Toluca, Mexico, children eat sweet, ripe bananas.

Page 6: In Scotland, a toddler tastes—and wears—chocolate.

Page 7: Two English schoolgirls stop for a spaghetti lunch.

Page 8: Young children in Hong Kong say grace before eating.

Page 9: These boys in Morocco, in northwest Africa, use their hands to eat couscous topped with vegetables and meat.

Page 10: Women on a trip to Antarctica eat lunch on their ship.

Page 11: Kids on a field trip to the George Washington Carver National Monument in Missouri take a lunch break.

Page 12: A student on the go in Ho Chi Minh City, Vietnam, eats a quick snack.

Page 13: In Puttaparthi, India, a boy brings home a basket of tomatoes to cook.

Page 14: A teacher shows off the vegetables she has grown in Malawi, a country in southeastern Africa.

Page 15: A woman in Nigeria, in West Africa, removes cocoa beans from their pods.

Page 16: It's time to chop onions in this kitchen in Chisinau, Moldova.

Page 17: Women in Ghana, a country in West Africa, make smoked herring on a grill.

Page 18: At a shelter for homeless children in Bangkok, Thailand, children get a hot meal.

Page 19: A teacher in Fort Simpson, in the Northwest Territories, shows native Canadian girls how to make hot dogs covered with bannock, a kind of bread.

Page 20: A child from a hill tribe in Tamil Nadu, India, sits down to eat.

Page 21: In Paris, France, a mother and son share some mealtime fun.

A Note to Adults on Sharing This Book

Help your child become a lifelong reader. Read this book together, taking turns as you both read out loud. Look over the photographs and choose your favorites. Sound out new words and come back to them later for review. Then try these "extensions"—activities that extend the experience of reading and build discussion and problem-solving skills.

Talk about Eating

All around the world, you can find people eating. Discuss with your child the kinds of foods people eat in different countries. Where do you get the food you eat? Where do people in other parts of the world get their food? What ways of preparing food are shown in this book?

Make a Food Chart

With your child, draw pictures of the foods you both love to eat. Find pictures of your favorite foods in magazines. Then find out where your favorite foods fit on the food pyramid. Which of your favorite foods should you eat less of—or more of—in order to be healthy?

The Food Pyramid

Fats, Oils & Sugars
less than 1 serving per day

Milk, Cheese & Yogurt
Group
2–3 servings

Meat, Poultry, Fish, Eggs,
Dry Beans & Nut Group
2–3 servings

Vegetable Group
3–5 servings

Fruit Group
2–4 servings

Bread, Pasta,
Cereal & Rice
Group

6–11 servings